ALL OUR COMMUNITIES

YOU'RE PART OF A NATIONAL COMMUNITY!

T0009988

BY THERESA EMMINIZER

Gareth Stevens
PUBLISHING

Please visit our website, www.garethstevens.com. For a free color catalog of all our high-quality books, call toll free 1-800-542-2595 or fax 1-877-542-2596.

Cataloging-in-Publication Data

Names: Emminizer, Theresa.
Title: You're part of a national community! / Theresa Emminizer.
Description: New York : Gareth Stevens Publishing, 2020. | Series: All our communities | Includes glossary and index.
Identifiers: ISBN 9781538245330 (pbk.) | ISBN 9781538245354 (library bound) | ISBN 9781538245347 (6 pack)
Subjects: LCSH: Citizenship–Juvenile literature. | Community life–Juvenile literature. | Communities–Juvenile literature.
Classification: LCC JF801.E463 2020 | DDC 323.6–dc23

Published in 2020 by
Gareth Stevens Publishing
111 East 14th Street, Suite 349
New York, NY 10003

Designer: Sarah Liddell
Editor: Theresa Emminizer

Photo credits: cover, pp. 1, 15 Africa Studio/Shutterstock.com; background texture used throughout april70/Shutterstock.com; papercut texture used throughout Paladjai/Shutterstock.com; p. 5 Robert Kneschke/Shutterstock.com; pp. 7, 21 Monkey Business Images; pp. 9, 13 Rob Crandall/Shutterstock.com; p. 11 realpeople/Shutterstock.com; p. 17 Olena Yakobchuk/Shutterstock.com; p. 19 Oksana Shufrych/Shutterstock.com.

Printed in the United States of America

Some of the images in this book illustrate individuals who are models. The depictions do not imply actual situations or events.

CPSIA compliance information: Batch #CW20GS: For further information contact Gareth Stevens, New York, New York at 1-800-542-2595.

CONTENTS

Boldface words appear in the glossary.

What Is a Nation?

A nation is a community of people who share a government. As an American, you are part of the community of the United States. We may speak different languages and have different beliefs, but we are all a part of one national community.

Your National Community

A community is a group of people living and working together. Every person living in America is part of your national community. That means government leaders like the president, government workers like mail carriers, and everyday **citizens** like your friends and neighbors.

Citizens' Roles

America is a **representative** democracy. That means the government is run by the people. Citizens choose how the nation will be run by voting for leaders to represent them in government. Each citizen has a voice and a special **role** to play.

Where Do You Fit?

Even if you aren't old enough to vote, you have a role in your national community. Our nation is founded on a set of values: **freedom**, equality, and **justice**. As a citizen, you can do your part by helping to **uphold** these values.

11

What Freedom Means

Freedom means having the right to speak your mind, believe what you want to, and make your own decisions. You can help uphold freedom by listening to and respecting the ideas and beliefs of others even if you don't agree with them.

Working for Equality

In our national community, everyone is equal. We all have rights, no matter your skin color, abilities, **gender**, or where you live. Respect and **protect** the rights of community members who are different from you.

Justice for All

Justice means treating everyone fairly. All members of our national community should be treated with respect and given the chance to learn and do well. You can uphold the value of justice by acting kindly toward others and being a good sport.

The Common Good

Being a part of a national community means thinking about what is best for everyone, not just yourself. You can work for the common good by following rules and laws, telling the truth, and caring about what happens to others.

Get Started!

The greatest leaders in American history were citizens who tried to make their national community a better place for everyone. You have the power to make a difference too. The things you say and do today can help build a stronger national community tomorrow!

GLOSSARY

citizen: someone who lives in a country legally and has certain rights

freedom: the power to do what you would like to do

gender: the state of being seen as a boy or girl

justice: fairness

protect: to keep safe

representative: standing for a group of people

role: the part a person plays

uphold: to strengthen something or keep it going

FOR MORE INFORMATION

BOOKS

Boothroyd, Jennifer. *What Is Citizenship?* Minneapolis, MN: Lerner Publishing Group, 2016.

James, Emily. *How to Be a Good Citizen*. North Mankato, MN: Capstone Press, 2017.

WEBSITES

Duncksters Education Site
ducksters.com/history/us_government/democracy.php
Find out more about democracy and what it means.

Social Studies for Kids
socialstudiesforkids.com
Learn about the United States government and how it works.

INDEX